CW01183904

Original title:
Where Magic Lives

Copyright © 2024 Creative Arts Management OÜ
All rights reserved.

Author: Milo Harrington
ISBN HARDBACK: 978-9916-88-856-8
ISBN PAPERBACK: 978-9916-88-857-5

## **The Spellbound Grove**

In the heart of the trees, magic flows,
Whispers of secrets the soft breeze knows.
Moonlight drapes gently, shadows embrace,
A dance of the spirits, a mystical space.

Crisp leaves underfoot, a soft, hushed sound,
Where enchantment lingers and dreams are found.
Stars peer through branches, a sparkling gleam,
In the spellbound grove, we wander and dream.

## Tales from the Forgotten

Old stone walls hold stories untold,
Echoes of laughter, adventures bold.
Dusty tomes whisper in quiet repose,
In the hearts of the brave, the past overflows.

Figures in shadows weave patterns of yore,
A tapestry woven of legends galore.
With each turn of the page, we step back in time,
In tales from the forgotten, our spirits climb.

## The Luminescent Realm

In a world where the colors ignite,
Vibrant hues dance in the heart of the night.
Crystals above twinkle bright as a star,
In the luminescent realm, nothing is far.

Rivers of light flow, tranquil and clear,
A symphony of shimmer, enchanting and near.
Creatures of wonder roam wide and free,
In this luminous land, pure ecstasy.

## **Whims of the Wind**

The wind carries whispers of dreams yet to soar,
Tickling the leaves and knocking on doors.
Each breeze is a story, each gust a thrill,
In the whims of the wind, magic does spill.

Dancing in circles, leaves swirl and play,
Bringing the promise of a bright new day.
With each gentle sigh, the skies softly bend,
In the arms of the breezes, hearts start to mend.

## **Lullabies of the Fabled Forest**

In the heart of the woods so deep,
Whispers of magic gently creep.
Stars twinkle like fireflies bright,
Guiding lost dreams through the night.

Leaves rustle softly in the breeze,
Crickets play their serenade with ease.
Moonbeams dance on the forest floor,
Each shadow hides a secret door.

Echoes of laughter fill the air,
Nature hums with a tender care.
Cloaked in mist, ancient trees stand,
Guardians of tales from a forgotten land.

Close your eyes, and take a flight,
Through the lullabies of the night.
In this haven, let your spirit soar,
In the fabled forest, forevermore.

## **A Canvas of Shimmering Dreams**

Brushstrokes of color fill the sky,
Swirling wishes as the night goes by.
Stars are splattered like paint on dark,
Lighting pathways where visions spark.

Clouds drift softly, a gentle parade,
In this canvas where dreams are made.
Each hue whispers secrets untold,
Of adventures waiting, bold and gold.

A symphony of night unfolds,
In shades of silver, blue, and gold.
Close your eyes, let your heart explore,
In this realm where souls can soar.

Awake the dreams that long to gleam,
In a world alive with shimmering dream.
With every stroke, paint your own fate,
In this landscape, it's never too late.

## Echoes of a Forgotten Spell

In shadows deep where whispers sway,
A magic lost, in dusk's decay.
Once vibrant words that danced in light,
Now linger faint in the silent night.

The echoes call, a haunting tune,
Of dreams once bright beneath the moon.
An ancient charm, now wrapped in fog,
Haunts the stillness like a lost dog.

**Crystalline Paths through the Unknown**

Beneath the stars, the paths unfold,
In crystal shards, a tale retold.
Each step we take, a spark ignites,
Guiding souls through endless nights.

The mountains hum a secret song,
To wanderers who've journeyed long.
In every glint, a world awaits,
As fate entwines through open gates.

## The Luminescent Glade

In the glade where fireflies dance,
A thousand lights in a trance.
The trees stand tall, their branches bare,
Whispering hope in the midnight air.

Moonbeams wane on the softest ground,
Where dreams awaken, safe and sound.
Every shadow a sigh of relief,
In this haven beyond all grief.

## **Guardians of the Fabled Forest**

Deep within the emerald maze,
Ancient ones guard secrets, ablaze.
With eyes like stars and hearts of gold,
They watch the tales of time unfold.

Through tangled vines, their wisdom flows,
In every heartbeat, a mystery grows.
They keep the balance, the dawn, the dusk,
In whispered oaths, in dreams, they trust.

## The Luminous Threshold

At dawn's first light, we stand so bold,
With dreams aglow, and hearts of gold.
A path ahead, where shadows play,
We tread the dawn, embracing day.

Through whispered winds, our spirits soar,
A beckoning call from distant shore.
With every step, a spark ignites,
In this bright world, our hope ignites.

## **Enigmas of the Mind's Eye**

In quiet corners, secrets weave,
The mind's vast realms, we dare believe.
Reflections dance in the twilight haze,
Where thoughts entwine in endless maze.

Lost in dreams that twist and turn,
A flicker of truth, a hidden yearn.
Each shadow holds a story's thread,
In the mind's eye, all is said.

## **Tales of the Wistful**

Beneath the stars, the night unfolds,
Stories linger, softly told.
Of love and loss, of hope and grace,
In every tale, we find our place.

The moonlight whispers, memories dear,
Echoes of laughter, shed a tear.
In wistful dreams, we softly sway,
United by the stories we say.

## The Ethereal Voyage

Set sail on waves of twilight mist,
Where shadows dance and dreams exist.
With every heartbeat, the cosmos calls,
As stardust woven, in silence falls.

Each star a guide, through realms unknown,
In this vast sea, we find our own.
Together we drift, through time and space,
In the ethereal voyage, we embrace.

## **Chasing Celestial Beams**

In skies of blue, we chase the light,
Through whispers soft, the stars ignite.
With every step, the shadows flee,
We dance along with destiny.

The moon casts dreams on silver streams,
While time unravels in our schemes.
We reach for heights, where spirits soar,
In realms unknown, forevermore.

The dawn awakens with a glow,
As morning sings of what we know.
In every heart, a spark, a gleam,
Together, we are chasing beams.

So take my hand, let journeys blend,
With cosmic trails that never end.
Through galaxies, our spirits race,
In love's embrace, we find our place.

**The Fountain of Reveries**

In twilight's hush, the fountain flows,
Where dreams alight in soft repose.
With every drop, a story weaves,
In whispered secrets, hope believes.

The water dances, crystal clear,
Reflecting visions held so dear.
In echoes soft, the past awakes,
A tapestry of wishes makes.

Beneath the boughs, the shadows play,
As thoughts drift by like clouds in May.
Each splash, a promise, gently spun,
In this fair realm, our hearts are one.

So pause a while, let time elapse,
In this oasis, find your maps.
The fountain waits with arms outspread,
To greet the dreams that linger, bled.

# Mosaic of the Enchanted

Beneath the stars, a canvas bright,
Each fragment shines, a piece of night.
In colors bold, our stories blend,
A tapestry that knows no end.

The forest whispers, secrets shared,
In every leaf, the magic bared.
A door to worlds beyond our gaze,
Where wonders bloom in mystic ways.

Each step unveils a brand new view,
A swirling dance of shades and hue.
The nightingale sings soft and sweet,
In harmony, our hearts compete.

So wander deep, let spirits rise,
In every breath, the world surprise.
In this mosaic, love's refrain,
Enchanted dreams will still remain.

## **When Stars Forget**

In silent nights, when stars forget,
The stories spun, the dreams we set.
In shadows deep, where echoes sigh,
We search the skies, but still, they lie.

The moonlight wanes, a fading gleam,
As twilight steals away our dream.
Yet in our hearts, the fire stays,
A flicker soft, through endless days.

We'll gather hope, stitch light anew,
In quiet moments, hearts will view.
For every star that drifts away,
Another dawn will find its way.

So let us walk this path as one,
When stars forget, we'll still have sun.
Together, we will light the night,
With love aglow, our guiding light.

## Visions in the Mist

Amid the fog, shadows creep,
Whispers of secrets that silence keep.
Glimmers of light in twilight's breath,
Unravel the tales from beyond death.

Figures sway in a dreamy haze,
Lost in their own enchanted maze.
Each step taken, a story spun,
In the realm where the waking's done.

Nature's murmurs, soft and low,
Guide the heart where wild winds blow.
In every sigh, a memory traced,
In the mist, time is effaced.

Holding dreams as the night unfolds,
Visions of magic, silently told.
In the fog, we find our way,
To realms where light and shadow play.

## The Canvas of Night

Stars like jewels on velvet spread,
Cradle the stories of days long dead.
Moonlight dances on ancient trees,
Whispers of night carried by the breeze.

Brush of darkness, art divine,
In the stillness, the shadows twine.
Each heartbeat echoes, a silent hymn,
Within the night, senses brim.

Neon dreams awake in the dark,
Flickering sparks, each one a spark.
Painted skies tell tales of old,
In every hue, a wonder bold.

Amid the stars, mystery lies,
Under the canvas, our spirit flies.
The beauty of night invites us near,
To behold the magic we hold dear.

## Dances of the Faery Folk

In moonlit glen where shadows play,
Faery folk dance at the close of day.
With twinkling eyes and laughter bright,
They weave the magic of the night.

Whirls of color in graceful flight,
Nestled softly in silver light.
They beckon hearts to join the spell,
Where dreams ignited in laughter dwell.

With petals soft, they tread the ground,
A symphony of joy and sound.
Each step taken, a flicker of glee,
In the fairytale glade, set free.

The rhythm calls from deep within,
As night wraps all in its gentle skin.
Dance with the faery folk tonight,
Embrace the wonder, feel the light.

# **The Enigma of Solstice**

When shadows stretch and daylight wanes,
The solstice whispers ancient gains.
Time sways gently on a hidden thread,
In the dance of warmth, the cold is shed.

Wrapped in mysteries, both far and near,
Embodied tales that draw us here.
Sun and moon in a graceful fight,
Weaves of darkness, tapestry of light.

Echoes of seasons, pulse of the earth,
Celebrations rise for the day's rebirth.
With every tilt of the sky, we find,
Secrets revealed, beautifully entwined.

The enigma speaks in silent tones,
Awakening dreams in ancient bones.
As nature shifts, we too align,
In the heart of the solstice, divine.

## **The Melody of Secrets**

Whispers in the twilight air,
Softly dance, secrets share.
A tune that lingers, deep and rare,
In shadows where no one dares.

Echoes fade, yet hearts remain,
In silence, we feel the strain.
Notes of love, a sweet refrain,
Carried forth like a gentle rain.

In the dark, the melodies weave,
Threads of hope, we believe.
Each chord a memory to grieve,
Amongst the stars, we conceive.

Underneath the moonlit glow,
A secret's song begins to flow.
In every heart, a truth we know,
The melody of dreams will grow.

## The Garden of Forgotten Dreams

In a corner, where shadows fall,
Whispers of dreams, they gently call.
A garden of hope, both big and small,
With petals soft, they thrill us all.

Each flower blooms, a tale to tell,
Of wishes cast in evening's spell.
In the silence, secrets dwell,
Nurtured where memories swell.

Time has faded, yet they remain,
Each fragrance a soft, sweet pain.
Where dreams were lost, they still retain,
The echoes of love's soft refrain.

Among the leaves, the past awakes,
In quiet sighs, the heart still aches.
Through tangled vines, the hope remakes,
The dreams we hold, the joy that shakes.

# Harmonics of Enchantment

In twilight's embrace, we find a tune,
That dances beneath the watchful moon.
Harmonies rise, like flowers in bloom,
Enchantment swirls in the evening's room.

Notes unfold like wings in flight,
Crafting magic in the night.
Every breath feels pure delight,
As shadows waltz, keeping sight.

The world transforms with each soft chord,
In melodies where dreams are stored.
Echoes of laughter, love restored,
In this place, our souls are poured.

A symphony of stars above,
Whispers of memory, pain, and love.
Cascading notes like falling dove,
In this realm, we learn to move.

## Curiosities of the Ether

In the realm of dreams unknown,
Curiosities of life are sown.
Ideas dance, quietly shown,
In whispers carried by the wind's tone.

Mysterious worlds wait to explore,
Hidden secrets behind each door.
Voices beckon from the shore,
A gentle call, we can't ignore.

As stardust weaves through cosmic space,
Every thought finds its rightful place.
In the ether, we embrace,
The wonders time cannot erase.

With open hearts, we soar so high,
Through realms where dreams and spirits lie.
Infinite tales, and yet we shy,
To seek the truth beneath the sky.

## **Enchanted Whispers**

In a forest where shadows dance,
Whispers weave through branches bare,
Soft secrets brush the night,
Carried gently on the air.

Moonlit paths where dreams collide,
Echoes linger, hearts entwine,
Every step, a tale to tell,
Magic flows like vintage wine.

Leaves murmur with soft delight,
Stars above wink in reply,
The world breathes in hushed tones,
As time slips by, we sigh.

Underneath the ancient trees,
We find solace, pure and bright,
In enchanted whispers wrapped,
We embrace the velvet night.

## **Secrets of the Starlit Grove**

Beneath the velvet skies so wide,
Secrets stir and softly glow,
In the heart of the starlit grove,
Where ancient dreams begin to flow.

Crickets play a gentle tune,
Filling the night with sweet refrain,
Among the shadows, magic breathes,
In every line drawn by the rain.

Glowing fireflies dance like gems,
Illuminating paths unknown,
Each twinkle holds a whispered truth,
In this sacred space we've grown.

As we wander through the night,
Hand in hand, our spirits free,
Unraveling the woven threads,
Of secrets shared, just you and me.

## **Beneath the Silver Canopy**

Beneath the silver canopy high,
Where moonlight kisses every leaf,
We linger while the world holds still,
Embracing moments, sweet and brief.

The breeze carries songs of old,
Whispers wrapped in softest light,
Nature's breath, a lullaby,
Guiding dreams throughout the night.

Shadows dance with a gentle grace,
Silhouettes against the glow,
In this space of quiet peace,
We find solace, and time slows.

Cradled close in nature's arms,
Together lost, yet found as one,
Underneath this silver sky,
Our hearts beat, like a drum.

## **The Alchemist's Eden**

In a garden where wonders bloom,
The alchemist softly stirs,
With every petal, a hidden truth,
Crafted softly in delicate murmurs.

Sunlight spills on whispered spells,
Dancing across the vibrant hues,
Each leaf holds a tale untold,
Each blossom, secrets to peruse.

Golden elixirs kissed by dew,
Transforming moments into dreams,
In this Eden, time's fingers weave,
Life's essence flows like silver streams.

With a touch, the world ignites,
Magic lingers on every breath,
The alchemist conjures delight,
In this paradise, life transcends death.

# Reflections in the Enchanted Pool

Beneath the stars, the waters gleam,
A mirror holds a whispered dream,
Ripples skimming on the hue,
A dance of shadows, light breaks through.

Moonlit petals float in grace,
Silhouettes in their soft embrace,
Echoes rise from depths below,
Where secrets of the night may flow.

The willow bows to hear a tale,
Of lovers lost in twilight pale,
Each drop a story waits to tell,
A heartbeat lost, a wishing well.

Silent wishes brush the shore,
Carried by winds forevermore,
In the enchanted pool they lie,
Reflections of a fading sigh.

## The Secrets of the Ancient Grove

Upon the path where shadows weave,
The ancient grove begins to thieve,
Whispers curl around the bark,
Each rustling leaf, a hidden spark.

Time stands still within this realm,
Nature's grip, a steady helm,
Roots entwined with stories old,
In emerald hues, the past unfolds.

Sunlight dances through the leaves,
Where wisdom blooms and truth believes,
Branches cradle every sigh,
In silent knowledge, ages lie.

The ancient grove takes hold of dreams,
As time flows softly in its streams,
Here mysteries and tales converge,
In leafy arms, the spirits urge.

# Beyond the Veil of Reality

A curtain drawn, the world shifts light,
Enigma thrives in shadows bright,
Thoughts collide like waves at sea,
Beyond the veil, the truth is free.

Glimmers dance on edges frail,
A tapestry of hope set sail,
With every heartbeat, worlds collide,
In whispered dreams, we cannot hide.

Stars align with fate's embrace,
Each moment holds a sacred space,
Through every thought, a pathway glows,
Where nothing's certain, all things flow.

Beyond this veil, reality bends,
Where time's illusion softly mends,
With each new dawn, the mystery swells,
In realms where silence softly tells.

## The Heartbeat of the Mystic Vale

In twilight's grasp, where echoes play,
The mystic vale wakes at the end of day,
Each thrum of life entwined with lore,
A heartbeat pulses, forevermore.

Whispers rise from the rustling trees,
Carried softly on the breeze,
In every sigh, a legend breathes,
The vale conceals what love believes.

Moonlit shadows weave a song,
Where all the dreamers come along,
Hand in hand, they drift and sway,
To the rhythm of the night's ballet.

In this vale of magic's breath,
Life dances close to thoughts of death,
Each heartbeat tells of dreams fulfilled,
In the mystic vale, our souls are thrilled.

## **A Symphony of Illusions**

In whispers soft the echoes play,
A dance of light, a shadow's sway.
Notes of dream drift through the night,
Wrapped in tales of wrong and right.

Colors blend, a canvas bright,
Fragments lost in fading light.
The heartstrings pull, a tug of fate,
Caught between and in debate.

Notes that linger in the air,
Fractured moments, rare and fair.
In this symphony, we find
A melody that intertwines.

As illusions swirl around our feet,
Each heartbeat sings a tune discreet.
In the silence, we can hear
The whispers drawing ever near.

## Underneath the Gossamer Veil

Beneath the veil, the secrets lie,
Where starlight births a midnight sigh.
Each thread a story, soft and pure,
Weaving dreams that always endure.

The moonlight kisses every seam,
In twilight's hours, we're lost in dream.
With every fold, a breath of grace,
In this embrace, we find our place.

Time drips slowly, shadows dance,
Caught in a timeless, tender trance.
Gossamer whispers brush our skin,
Inviting all the light within.

And in that hush, we find our way,
A promise of a brand new day.
Underneath the veil we stand,
Together here, hand in hand.

## Echoes of the Past

In twilight's glow, the shadows creep,
Whispers of memories softly seep.
Ghosts of laughter fill the air,
Each echo carries timeless care.

Rustling leaves, a familiar song,
Tales of right and tales of wrong.
Fading footprints on the ground,
In every step, the lost are found.

The heart remembers, the soul will yearn,
From every lesson, there's much to learn.
In the stillness, we recall
Every rise, each gentle fall.

Yet as we journey through the night,
We chase the dawn, we seek the light.
Echoes guide us, strong and vast,
Leading us through the shadowed past.

## Charmed Silhouettes

In the twilight, silhouettes dance,
Shadows twirl in a timeless trance.
Beneath the starlit, velvet sky,
Dreams take flight, ready to fly.

Each figure holds a story true,
In whispers shared, between the two.
Their laughter rings, a sweet refrain,
Resonating through joy and pain.

With every turn, a spark ignites,
Charmed by the warmth of fleeting nights.
Together they weave a tapestry,
Of love and hope, wild and free.

So let them dance, these shadows bright,
In perfect harmony, pure delight.
For in their waltz, we see the best,
Charmed silhouettes, their hearts at rest.

## The Lure of Hidden Doors

In shadows deep, a whisper calls,
Through ivy wrapped and ancient walls.
Secrets lie beyond our gaze,
Where time stands still in twilight's haze.

A creaking hinge, a glint of gold,
Adventures wait, their stories bold.
With bated breath, we take the leap,
Into the dreams that linger deep.

Each door we find, a choice to make,
The path unfolds, a life to stake.
In hidden realms, our spirits soar,
To worlds unknown, behind each door.

So let us roam, our hearts set free,
In the lure of doors we cannot see.
Awake the magic, breathe it in,
For every ending sparks a new begin.

## **Reflections of the Otherworld**

In twilight's glow, the mirrors gleam,
Reflecting shades of dreams unseen.
The otherworld calls, a soft embrace,
Where time and space find their own grace.

With silver streams and haunting light,
Echoes whisper through the night.
A dance of shadows, a silent song,
In the mirror's depth, we feel we belong.

Faces shift like clouds above,
A glimpse of past, a touch of love.
We stand in awe, lost in the trance,
In every flicker, a mystic dance.

So heed the call, take the chance,
In reflections soft, let spirits dance.
For in the otherworld, we find our part,
A journey woven in the heart.

## **Guardians of the Veil**

Within the mists, the guardians stand,
With watchful eyes, and outstretched hands.
They guard the secrets of the night,
With gentle strength, they hold the light.

Through ancient woods and whispered air,
They weave the threads of magic rare.
With heartbeats soft, they guide our way,
Beneath the stars, where shadows play.

In every sigh, a tale untold,
Of spirits brave and hearts of gold.
The veil between worlds, they tend with care,
For in their watch, our dreams are rare.

So walk with faith, through dark and deep,
For guardians watch, their vigil keep.
With every heartbeat, feel the flow,
Of magic's breath, in shadows known.

## **The Melody of Lost Spells**

In quiet groves where spirits dwell,
There lingers still a magic well.
With notes of old and whispers soft,
The melody of spells takes off.

Each strum of breeze, each rustle leaf,
Carries tales of joy and grief.
In every sound, an echo's dance,
Our hearts ignite, entranced, in trance.

Old tomes forgotten, dust collects,
Yet in our souls, their power reflects.
For every song, a charm is cast,
Connecting futures, present, past.

So listen close, to nature's tune,
The melody hums beneath the moon.
In every spell that time has lost,
A world of wonder waits, embossed.

## **Sirens in the Mist**

In twilight's arms, they softly sing,
Voices echo, a haunting ring.
Misty veils obscure the shore,
Luring sailors evermore.

Waves crash gently, secrets shared,
Crashing hearts, a love ensnared.
Figures dance in foggy gloom,
Leaving shadows to consume.

A melody that stirs the soul,
Yearning hearts are lost, not whole.
Fleeting whispers through the night,
Draw them closer, out of sight.

As dawn unfolds, their magic fades,
The sirens' song, a memory made.
Yet on the sea, dreams still persist,
In the echoes of the mist.

## **Wonders of the Evernight**

Beneath a sky of endless stars,
Dreams take flight, no bounds, no bars.
In the stillness, shadows weave,
Tales of magic, hearts believe.

Whispers float on midnight air,
Secrets hidden, so rare, so fair.
Glimmers dance on dewy grass,
Moments fleeting, yet they last.

Time stands still in the deep blue,
Mysteries wrapped in moonlit hue.
Every glance reveals a spark,
Illuminating dreams in dark.

As night unfolds, more wonders soar,
Endless stories, forever more.
Together, they paint the skies,
In the dance of night's disguise.

## **Tides of Enchantment**

Waves of silver kiss the shore,
Whispers carried from the moor.
Each tide brings a tale anew,
Of longing hearts and skies of blue.

Moonlit paths glow softly bright,
Guiding souls through endless night.
In the rhythm, secrets dwell,
Of love and loss, of heaven and hell.

Oceans swell with timeless dreams,
Flowing gently, as life seems.
Nature's canvas etched in foam,
Each wave a heart, a wish, a home.

With every ebb, the spirits sigh,
Tales of lovers who dared to fly.
Forever caught in dance of fate,
In the tides, they celebrate.

## Portraits of the Arcane

Brushstrokes shimmer in the night,
Casting shadows with their light.
Eyes that hold the stars' embrace,
Capturing time in every trace.

Whispers of magic flicker slow,
In every portrait, tales bestow.
Colors bleed, a vivid dream,
Where reality's not what it seems.

Figures linger, secrets tease,
Captured still in softest breeze.
What stories lie behind each gaze?
In the arcane, time betrays.

Galleries filled with vibrant lore,
Echoes of the ages roar.
Each portrait sings a world so vast,
Inviting hearts to roam the past.

## Realm of the Unseen

In shadows deep where whispers dwell,
The secrets hide, they weave a spell.
With silent steps, the night unfolds,
A tapestry of stories told.

Beneath the stars, a clock ticks slow,
Time drifts like mists that softly flow.
In corners dark, a flicker gleams,
As dreams collide with quiet schemes.

The air is thick with unsaid lore,
Each breath a chance to seek and soar.
Through veils of night, the echoes call,
Unlock the door, embrace it all.

In twilight's grip, the unseen dance,
With every glance, a fleeting chance.
The realm of thoughts, a boundless sea,
Where all that's lost will find its key.

# The Sorcerer's Garden

In blooms of light, the shadows play,
Where magic stirs in bright array.
With petals soft, the secrets thrive,
In this enchanted garden, alive.

A whisper floats, the winds embrace,
With every breath, a hidden grace.
The herbs that twine, the fruits that gleam,
All offer paths to spark a dream.

Beneath the moon, the colors swirl,
As fireflies dance in twinkling whirl.
In every leaf, a story grows,
Of ancient ties and mystic flows.

Here spells are cast with gentle hands,
In harmony where nature stands.
The sorcerer's heart finds peace anew,
In every hue, a magic true.

## **Threads of Wonder**

In woven strands of time and fate,
The moments shift, they contemplate.
Each thread a tale, a life unfurls,
In patterns rich, the world swirls.

A tapestry of joys and fears,
Intertwined with laughter, tears.
In every knot, a lesson learned,
In every twist, a heart still burned.

The loom of life, a rhythmic weave,
In every pause, we must believe.
Through golden hues and shadows cast,
We stitch the future, learn from the past.

With nimble hands, we craft our dreams,
In colors bright, in quiet themes.
Threads of wonder, a tapestry spun,
In each creation, we are one.

## Beneath the Silver Moon

In gentle glow where stillness breathes,
The silver moon through branches weaves.
With every beam, the soft night sings,
A lullaby of whispered things.

The world beneath, a canvas blank,
With shadows deep, in silence, frank.
Each step a wish, a secret shared,
In moonlight's glow, our hearts laid bare.

The stars above, a scattered fleet,
With tales of love on rhythmic beat.
In this serene and tranquil night,
We find our way, our hopes ignite.

Beneath the moon, we dream and roam,
In every heart, we find our home.
The silver light, a guiding tune,
We dance together, beneath the moon.

## **Whispers of Enchantment**

In twilight's haze, dreams softly weave,
A melody of night, hearts believe.
Moonlight dances on the silver stream,
Echoes of magic in every dream.

Glimmers of hope in the darkened wood,
Whispers of love where the wild things stood.
Stars align in a cosmic embrace,
Guiding lost souls to a sacred space.

With every breath, a secret to share,
Nature's soft sighs are beyond compare.
In the stillness, we find our way,
Through shadows and light, come what may.

The universe hums, a soft lullaby,
Awakening wonders that never die.
In silence, we hear the world's sweet breath,
A symphony woven in life and death.

## **Secrets Among the Stars**

In the velvet sky, wishes take flight,
Stars whisper secrets in the deep night.
Each twinkle holds tales of longing and fate,
Connecting the hearts of those who wait.

Nebulas bloom in a cosmic dance,
Infinite wonders ignite the chance.
Galaxies turning, both distant and clear,
Echoing dreams that drift ever near.

Constellations map the paths we choose,
In the quiet night, we cannot lose.
Time slips away like grains of sand,
Beneath the starlight, hand in hand.

In cosmic silence, our spirits rise,
Sailing forever through endless skies.
Among the stars, we find our song,
In the universe vast, we all belong.

## The Alchemist's Dream

Amidst the shadows, a whisper takes form,
Alchemy brews in the mystic storm.
Turning lead to gold in moon's gentle light,
Crafting the dreams that dance in the night.

With ancient runes etched in the air,
Secrets unfold without a care.
Potions and spells conjure the unseen,
In the heart's cauldron, where hopes convene.

Each drop a story, each swirl a fate,
In the alchemist's hands, the world resonates.
Transmuting sorrow into blissful streams,
Awakening the soul to its glorious dreams.

In twilight's embrace, he seeks to create,
A tapestry woven from love, not hate.
For in every spark lies a path to explore,
The alchemist's dream opens every door.

## Echoes of the Enchanted

In gardens where the wild blossoms grow,
Echoes of laughter, soft winds that blow.
Nature sings songs of a bygone time,
Whispers of magic in rhythm and rhyme.

The willows sway with tales of the past,
In shadows of stories that forever last.
Moonbeams shimmer on a glistening lake,
Reflecting the dreams that we dare to make.

A flicker of fireflies dances in the air,
Spinning enchantment beyond compare.
With each gentle breeze, a new chapter starts,
Binding our lives in mysterious arts.

In moments of still, let the echoes play,
Guiding our hearts in a wondrous display.
For in the enchanted, we find our way,
Carried on whispers that never decay.

## **Mysteries of the Ethereal Spring**

Beneath the veil of morning dew,
Awakens life in shades anew.
Soft whispers dance on gentle sighs,
A symphony of nature's ties.

Fluttering petals, hues so bright,
In fragrant gardens, pure delight.
The breeze carries secrets untold,
Of ancient dreams and hearts of gold.

Streams that shimmer in the light,
Reflecting wishes, pure and bright.
In every shadow, magic lingers,
As springtime's touch uncurls its fingers.

With every bloom, the world takes flight,
A canvas painted with delight.
Ethereal spirits weave their song,
In mysteries where we belong.

## **Lanterns of the Dreamweaver's Path**

Along the trail where dreams ignite,
Lanterns glow with soft, warm light.
They guide the souls who drift and roam,
To find their hearts, to find their home.

Each flicker tells a tale of old,
Of whispered hopes and dreams of gold.
The night unfolds in shades of grace,
As dreamers wander, find their place.

Stars above like diamonds shine,
In the realm where hearts align.
With every step, new worlds arise,
Beneath the vast and endless skies.

So follow the glow through night's embrace,
Where magic weaves in time and space.
For in the light, the heart can see,
The path of dreams, eternally.

# **The Spellbound Shoreline**

Waves that whisper secrets deep,
The shoreline sings as tides do sweep.
In salty air, the stories blend,
Of journeys taken, hearts to mend.

Footprints trace the sandy land,
Echoing dreams of hearts once planned.
Seagulls call in rhythmic flight,
Dancing on the edge of night.

The ocean's pulse, a soothing balm,
Imparts a sense of peace and calm.
With every crash, the waves implore,
The magic held along the shore.

As twilight falls, the stars ignite,
Reflecting love on waves so bright.
In this spellbound, timeless place,
The shoreline holds our dreams in grace.

## **Tales from the Whispering Woods**

In tangled roots where shadows blend,
The whispering woods, where secrets bend.
Each rustling leaf tells stories old,
Of laughter, loss, and hearts of gold.

Moonlight filters through the trees,
Carrying tales upon the breeze.
Where ancient spirits softly tread,
And every glance may be misread.

Crickets sing their twilight tune,
As fireflies dance beneath the moon.
The heart of nature breathes and sighs,
In every whisper, truth defies.

So wander deep, let shadows guide,
Through winding paths where dreams abide.
In whispering woods, you'll find your truth,
The ageless tales of love and youth.

## **Fables Born from Starlight**

In the quiet night, stars gleam bright,
Whispers of tales, taking flight.
Creatures of wonder, dreams unfold,
Fables spun from threads of gold.

Moonlit paths where secrets hide,
Guiding hearts with cosmic pride.
Each twinkle sparks, a story's tale,
A universe where wishes sail.

Through shimmering skies, we drift away,
Chasing the dawn of a new day.
With stardust kisses on our brow,
Fables born, alive somehow.

In twilight's hush, our spirits soar,
Fables igniting forevermore.
Let starlit dreams be our guide,
As we wander through time, side by side.

## The Wishing Well of Lost Dreams

In the forest deep, a well does sing,
Cradling hopes on a silver spring.
Coins of sorrow, wishes cast,
For dreams unkept, the shadows last.

Beneath the moon, softly it glows,
A haven where longing freely flows.
Old echoes dance with a gentle sigh,
As wishes bubble, never die.

Voices of yore whisper and plea,
When the sun sets, they long to be free.
Each wish a petal, floating on air,
Meandering softly, laying bare.

In the stillness, hope renews,
Amid fading fears, a path true.
From the depths, we learn to believe,
In the well of dreams, we weave.

## Echoes of Enchantment

In a glade where magic dwells,
The earth resounds with ancient bells.
Whispers weave through branches high,
Echoes hold tales and lullabies.

Here laughter mingles with the leaves,
In every rustle, the heart believes.
Footsteps of elves on paths unseen,
In soft twilight, they drift and gleam.

A spell of silver in the air,
Each breath a promise to repair.
With every heartbeat, truths unfold,
In echoes, the mysteries hold.

Where the moonlight paints the night,
Wonders awaken, hearts take flight.
In the whispers that softly call,
Enchantments linger, sweet and small.

## The Song of the Merrow's Lament

Beneath the waves, where shadows play,
The merrow sings by night and day.
A haunting tune of love's lost plight,
Rippling softly in the moonlight.

With ocean's breath, her sorrows sigh,
A melody for the waves to cry.
In coral halls, her heart does weep,
For promises that drifted deep.

Every note a tear well spent,
In the tide's embrace, her heart content.
Shadows dance where echoes swell,
Listening close to the merrow's spell.

Above the seas, the stars align,
Carrying tales, both yours and mine.
In every wave, her story's cast,
The song of longing shall forever last.

## The Language of Fireflies

In the night, they dance and glow,
Whispers of light, a soft tableau.
Magic spun in gentle flight,
Secrets shared in fleeting night.

They blink their tales, a silent song,
A flicker here, then they're gone.
In twilight's hush, a symphony,
Of shimmering dreams, wild and free.

Each spark a word, unspoken grace,
Guiding hearts to a sacred space.
With every flicker, hope ignites,
A language born of starry nights.

Beneath the moon, their stories weave,
We watch in awe, and we believe.
A chorus of light, in shadows cast,
They teach us love, as moments pass.

## Hidden in Twilight

As daylight fades, the world transforms,
A hush descends, the evening warms.
Shadows stretch in golden hues,
Secrets lie in the evening's blues.

Silent whispers fill the air,
Mysteries float with every prayer.
Beneath the stars, the heart takes flight,
Searching for truth hidden in night.

The forest breathes an ancient lore,
While time slows down, we seek for more.
Veils of dusk, where dreams entwine,
In twilight's grasp, our souls align.

A world unveiled by softest glow,
In stillness, let the silence flow.
For in this space, magic ignites,
Revealing wonders in moonlit sights.

## Enchanted Pathways

Through the woods, where secrets dwell,
Whispers of nature weave a spell.
Footsteps fall on mossy ground,
Ancient stories all around.

Sunbeams break through leafy crowns,
Painting gold on emerald towns.
Every turn, a tale to meet,
Where fairies dance and dreamers greet.

Petals flutter on gentle breeze,
A melody played among the trees.
The air is thick with fragrant lore,
An invitation to explore.

On enchanted pathways, lost we roam,
Finding magic, we call it home.
Each step taken leads us near,
To wonder's heart, forever clear.

## **The Chronicles of Fable**

In a world where legends dwell,
Stories rise, and shadows swell.
Each tale, a thread of woven dreams,
Life unfolds in vibrant themes.

Heroes brave, with hearts of fire,
Facing foes and climbing higher.
Myths and fables, old yet new,
Teach us lessons, bold and true.

Underneath the ancient skies,
The spirit of adventure flies.
With every page, we find our fate,
In whispered words, we resonate.

Chronicles penned with ink of stars,
A tapestry stitched with love and scars.
In every fable, truth emerges,
Guiding souls as fate converges.

## **Riddles of the Moonlight**

Beneath the silver glow, secrets confide,
Whispers of the night, where shadows reside.
Glimmers of truth dance on the gleam,
Lost in reflections of a half-formed dream.

Each twinkle a question, the stars softly sigh,
Echoes of laughter, a lullaby's cry.
The moon weaves its story on the darkened sea,
In riddles of light, what might we foresee?

Soft breezes carry the tales of the wise,
Searching for answers in luminous skies.
A labyrinth of wonders, pathways unfold,
In the heart of the night, mysteries told.

To wander is to ponder, to gaze is to see,
Veils of the cosmos whisper their plea.
As shadows embrace the coming dawn's fight,
We unravel the riddles of the moonlit night.

## **The Hidden Tapestry**

In threads of gold, stories entwine,
Patterns of time, woven divine.
Each stitch a memory, each knot a sigh,
The fabric of lives, no reason to lie.

Under the surface, colors collide,
Whispers of fate, where hopes do abide.
A tapestry rich, but hidden from view,
The art of existence, in shades old and new.

With every unravel, a tale to be told,
Laughter and heartache in fibers of bold.
A journey of souls, in silence they speak,
Threads of connection, the strong and the weak.

As we weave our own, let love be the guide,
In this grand design, we walk side by side.
Each life a strand, a spark in the night,
The hidden tapestry reveals its true light.

## Portals of Perception

Glimmering gates in the corners of thought,
Visions unfold in the battles we fought.
Mirrors reflect what the heart cannot see,
Unlocking the walls that we build to be free.

Through lenses of wonder, we search for the truth,
In colors of wisdom, we find our lost youth.
Every perspective a chance to expand,
Horizons awaken when we understand.

The world spins in ways both familiar and strange,
Chasing the echoes of moments that change.
With each shift we journey, embrace the unknown,
In portals of perception, our spirits have grown.

Embrace the unknown, let your vision transcend,
Connections await where the paths seem to blend.
For in every glance lies a universe bright,
In portals of perception, we find our own light.

## **Timeless Whispers**

In the hush of the night, echoes softly call,
Ancient voices sing, reminding us all.
From valleys of memory, stories arise,
Timeless whispers weave through the skies.

Moments like shadows, fleeting and fast,
Each heartbeat a stretch, a bridge to the past.
With each breath we take, threads of time blend,
In the whispers of ages, we learn to transcend.

The clock may keep ticking, but we hold the key,
To dance with the past, to set ourselves free.
With whispers as guides, we wander anew,
In timeless embrace, our spirits break through.

So listen intently, let silence bestow,
The treasures of wisdom, the seeds we can sow.
For in these soft murmurs, we find who we are,
Timeless whispers leading us, near and far.

## **Portals to the Unseen**

Through whispered winds the secrets flow,
In shadows deep where few dare go.
Mirrored realms that twist and bend,
Awaken dreams that never end.

With every step, the paths unfold,
A tapestry of tales retold.
Stars align in silent grace,
Unraveling the hidden space.

Voices echo from the past,
In time's embrace, forever cast.
Each portal glows, a guiding light,
Drawing souls from day to night.

So take a leap, embrace the call,
In unseen worlds, we rise and fall.
Together we shall wander free,
Explore the realms of mystery.

## The Garden of Forgotten Wishes

In the garden where dreams decay,
Petals whisper what hearts don't say.
Once bright hopes now fade and blend,
Among the shadows, they pretend.

Each blossom holds a tale untold,
Of love once warm, now icy cold.
Beneath the weeping willow's sigh,
Lie aspirations, buried high.

The fountain trickles lost desires,
While crickets serenade the fires.
In moonlit nights, they softly weep,
For promises they could not keep.

Yet in this place of fading light,
New wishes bloom, a wondrous sight.
From ashes rise, what once was gone,
In this garden, hope lives on.

## **Melodies of the Moonlit Meadow**

Beneath the stars, where shadows play,
The moonlit meadow holds its sway.
Whispers dance on gentle breeze,
As night awakens, hearts find ease.

Crickets sing a lullaby sweet,
Each note a memory, pure and neat.
Fireflies twinkle, a soft embrace,
Guiding wanderers to this place.

With every rustle, secrets share,
In this haven, devoid of care.
The melodies drift, lose their form,
In harmony, we feel the warm.

So linger long, let spirits soar,
In moonlit meadows, find the door.
To worlds where dreams continuously flow,
In this magical, twilight glow.

## Chronicles of the Twilight Kingdom

In twilight realms where shadows blend,
Awake the tales that never end.
A kingdom forged in whispered lore,
With ancient secrets at its core.

The castles rise beneath the skies,
Where dreams are spun with silver ties.
Each tower holds its story dear,
Of joy, of sorrow, hope, and fear.

From fading light to starlit hue,
The chronicles of old renew.
With every breath, we seek to find,
The legacy left far behind.

So venture forth, let courage beam,
In twilight's grasp, embrace the dream.
Together we'll pen our own refrain,
In this kingdom, love shall reign.

## A Dance with Shadows

In the twilight where secrets dwell,
Soft whispers weave a spell.
The shadows twirl, the candles sway,
In their embrace, night turns to day.

A moonlit stage, a fleeting glance,
Echoes of laughter, a ghostly dance.
They flicker, fade, in misty trails,
Chasing dreams as daylight fails.

Between the light and dark we roam,
Seeking solace, a place called home.
The dance continues, the echoes play,
In shadow's arms, we find our way.

So let us sway in the cool night air,
With every twirl, we shed our care.
Forever caught in twilight's hue,
A dance with shadows, just me and you.

# The Heart of the Mystic

Beneath the stars, the whispers rise,
A mystic's heart, where truth belies.
In quiet realms of thought and dream,
The universe flows like a shimmering stream.

With hands outstretched, we seek to find,
The secrets hidden within our mind.
Each pulse of magic, a sacred thread,
Connecting all, in silence spread.

Lost in the labyrinth of our fate,
We tread the path both wide and straight.
The heart beats steady, a timeless guide,
Through realms of wonder, we must abide.

In every heartbeat, in every breath,
We dance with life, we conquer death.
To follow whispers of wisdom true,
The heart of the mystic shines anew.

## **Palette of Illusions**

Colors blend in the twilight glow,
Painting dreams only artists know.
With every brush, a story unfold,
In hues of warmth and shades of cold.

Illusions dance in the morning light,
Whispers of truth, hiding from sight.
Each stroke a vision, a glimpse of fate,
In the palette's embrace, we contemplate.

The canvas stretches, inviting the mind,
With shadows lurking, and treasures to find.
In vibrant blurs, emotions collide,
A symphony of life, where spirits reside.

So let us create, in colors so vast,
A world of wonders, where memories cast.
With pencils and dreams, we sharpen our view,
In this palette of illusions, we paint anew.

## **The Dreamweaver's Song**

In the silence of night, the dreamers sigh,
As the dreamweaver whispers, the stars comply.
With threads of gold and silver spun,
They weave the tales that drift and run.

Each note a feather, soft and light,
Gliding softly through the night.
With every chord, the worlds align,
In the dreamweaver's song, all hearts entwine.

Through valleys deep and mountains high,
The melodies soar, they touch the sky.
In every heart, a rhythm grows,
As the dreamweaver sings, the magic flows.

So close your eyes, let the music play,
In the arms of dreams, we drift away.
With every whisper, a dream takes flight,
In the dreamweaver's song, all is right.

# The Keeper of Wonders

In a forest deep where shadows play,
The keeper of wonders hides away.
Whispers of magic in every breeze,
Secrets preserved among the trees.

A lantern glows with an eerie light,
Guiding lost souls through the night.
With every step, a story unfolds,
Of dreams and wishes, and truths untold.

Stars twinkle down through the leafy veil,
As the keeper spins a timeless tale.
Of treasures hidden and paths to roam,
In the heart of the woods, we find our home.

So heed the call of the ancient rhyme,
For wonders await in the arms of time.
Journey forth with a heart so bold,
And let the keeper's tales be told.

## Fables of the Unknown

In shadows cast by flickering flames,
Whispers of fables call by name.
Untold stories of the vast night,
Lurking just beyond our sight.

A traveler wanders, lost in thought,
Seeking the lessons that life has brought.
Each step unveils a hidden lore,
Of worlds unseen and opened doors.

In echoes of silence where secrets lie,
The fables of old begin to fly.
They dance like leaves in the autumn wind,
Telling of journeys where dreams rescind.

So listen closely to the quiet tune,
For in the dark, the fables bloom.
Embrace the whispers of what's yet to be,
And find the wonders that set you free.

## **Moonlit Reveries**

Beneath the moon's soft, silver glow,
Dreams awaken, silently flow.
Stars like diamonds on velvet skies,
Whispering secrets, where magic lies.

In moonlit reveries, we drift afar,
Guided by the light of a wandering star.
Each fleeting thought a delicate thread,
Woven with hopes, with things unsaid.

A gentle breeze carries a sweet refrain,
Of lost loves calling through the rain.
In this soft embrace, let your heart soar,
For in the night, we are forevermore.

So let us wander beneath this hue,
Where every moment feels fresh and new.
In moonlit reveries, we dare to dream,
Finding solace in the starlit gleam.

## **Echoing in the Ethereal**

In realms unseen, we take our flight,
Echoing whispers through the night.
Voices of ages, faint yet clear,
Guiding the lost, inspiring the near.

A chorus rises from the void,
Filling the silence once devoid.
With every tone, a story sings,
Of distant lands and forgotten things.

Between the stars, where shadows meld,
Echoes of the ethereal are held.
Each heartbeat bears the weight of time,
In the cosmic rhythm, an endless rhyme.

So seek the echoes, listen well,
In the beauty of silence, a story to tell.
For in the ethereal, we find our place,
With dreams intertwining in timeless grace.

## **Serendipity in Starlight**

Under a canvas of shimmering night,
Dreams dance softly in silvery light.
Whispers of fortune on the cool breeze,
Every heartbeat a sweet, gentle tease.

Stars collide in a cosmic embrace,
Tracing the paths of a wondrous chase.
In the silence, secrets unfold,
Moments of magic, stories retold.

Wandering souls find a spark,
Guided by shadows that leave their mark.
Life's little wonders, a shimmering thread,
Woven in starlight where dreams are spread.

In the night air, laughter ignites,
Promises bloom in the starry heights.
Embracing the beauty that's always near,
Finding serendipity, holding it dear.

# Harmonies of the Arcane

In twilight's grasp where shadows dwell,
Mysteries murmur, casting a spell.
Echoes of magic linger in air,
Whispers of wisdom, hidden and rare.

Chanting softly, the ancients unite,
Revealing secrets in the quiet night.
A symphony flows through the leaves,
Carving their tales in the heart of eves.

Stars align in a celestial dance,
Inviting souls to take a chance.
Threads of fate woven with care,
In the fabric of time that we all share.

So listen closely, hearts entwined,
In the harmonies that fate designed.
For in the arcane, we find our song,
A melody sweet where we all belong.

**The Hidden Lantern**

In a forgotten nook, where shadows play,
A lantern flickers, lighting the way.
It beckons softly with a warm glow,
Guiding lost souls through valleys below.

Rustling leaves tell tales of the past,
Echoes of laughter that once held fast.
The whispers of time linger and flow,
In the space where memories gently grow.

Secrets are kept in corners unseen,
The light reveals where we have been.
In its embrace, fears start to fade,
Illuminating paths that have been laid.

So follow the glow through night's deep fold,
A hidden lantern, worth more than gold.
For in the darkness, hope finds its space,
Guided by light, we all find our place.

## **Whispers of Ancient Woods**

In ancient woods where echoes dwell,
Nature unfolds her timeless spell.
Leaves murmur secrets of days gone by,
Beneath the vast and endless sky.

Branches arch with a knowing grace,
Cradling stories in their embrace.
A symphony sung by creatures small,
Ancient wisdom in each gentle call.

Thick moss carpets the forest floor,
A patchwork of life forevermore.
Each step a tribute to days of yore,
In every whisper, the woods restore.

So listen close, let your spirit roam,
In the sacred woods, you'll find your home.
For in the silence, peace will prevail,
In the whispers of nature, love will not fail.

## Shadows of the Enchanted Realm

In the hush of night, whispers call,
Shadows dance, they rise and fall.
Mysteries wrapped in silver light,
Stars above twinkle, growing bright.

Through the woods, a breeze does play,
Crickets sing, where fairies sway.
Lost in dreams, a path unfolds,
Secrets waiting to be told.

Glimmers bright in hidden nooks,
Magic sleeps in ancient books.
On this night, the heart will soar,
In the realm of evermore.

Join the dance, let spirits lead,
Follow whispers, sow the seed.
In shadows deep, enchantment's grace,
Find your home in this embrace.

## Dreams in the Twilight Mist

In the twilight, dreams arise,
Wrapped in fog beneath the skies.
Softly whispering, a tale begins,
Of secret hopes and whispered sins.

Petals fall from trees so old,
Stories woven, hearts unfold.
In misty realms where wishes tread,
Every thought like silk is spread.

Stars awaken in a dance,
Beckoning for a fleeting chance.
Floating whispers through the night,
Igniting souls with gentle light.

In this dreamscape, magic waits,
Open wide those guarded gates.
Let your spirit gently glide,
In twilight's arms, where dreams abide.

## When Fairies Dance by Moonlight

Beneath the moon's soft, silvery glow,
Fairies gather, a lively show.
Wings like gossamer, light as air,
In the stillness, they twirl and share.

Each little laugh a silvery sound,
Magic awakens, all around.
Petal skirts swirling in the breeze,
Nature watches through ancient trees.

Their joy is pure, their hearts take flight,
In the darkness, they bring delight.
Round and round, the circle spins,
Dreams take form, the night begins.

As dawn approaches, they shy away,
Leaving behind the night's ballet.
Yet if you listen, with bated breath,
You'll hear their laughter, defying death.

## **The Hidden Realm of Wonder**

In forests deep, where shadows play,
A hidden realm dreams night and day.
Twinkling lights in the cool night air,
Calling forth souls with tales to share.

Wonders linger beneath the trees,
Carried on every gentle breeze.
Lost in magic, where time stands still,
The heart awakens with a thrill.

Fables whispered by the brook,
In every corner, a story's nook.
In laughter's echo and silence sweet,
Life's enchantments linger, bittersweet.

Step lightly, friend, and you might find,
In every shadow, secrets bind.
Explore the magic, open your heart,
In this hidden realm, play your part.

## **The Secret of the Elders**

In whispers soft, the ancients speak,
Of tales long lost and wisdom's peak.
Beneath the trees, where shadows blend,
The echoes linger, never end.

A hidden path through tangled roots,
Reveals the truth in silent hoots.
With every rustle, secrets rise,
In the quiet, the past lies.

A flicker of light, a fleeting song,
Guides the dreamers who wander along.
To find the heart of ages past,
In the stillness, knowledge cast.

The elders watch, their eyes aglow,
Guarding tales of joy and woe.
For those who seek, the keys are near,
In nature's arms, the path is clear.

## Passages to Dreams

Through velvet nights, the starlight beams,
Unlocking doors to whispered dreams.
Each breath a journey, each sigh a flight,
Carried softly on wings of night.

In realms where shadows softly sway,
Our fantasies dance, never stray.
With every heartbeat, worlds align,
In the tapestry of the divine.

A river flows from mind to heart,
A sacred stream, where wonders start.
In dreams we paint with colors bold,
The stories waiting to be told.

As dawn approaches, visions fade,
Yet never lost, their magic laid.
With morning light, we find our way,
To live the dreams from night to day.

## **Twilight's Embrace**

When daylight bows to evening's grace,
The world transforms in twilight's embrace.
Colors blend in a gentle sigh,
As day begins its soft goodbye.

The stars emerge, like thoughts unspooled,
In silence, the heart is gently fueled.
As shadows stretch and whispers grow,
The night unfolds its tranquil glow.

In the cool air, a promise stirs,
Of secret hopes and gentle purrs.
With every moment, the night unveils,
The stories held in moonlit trails.

Twilight beckons, inviting dreams,
Where nothing is exactly as it seems.
In this calm, we find our place,
Wrapped in peace, in twilight's grace.

## **Shadows in the Moonlight**

Beneath the glow of silver beams,
Shadows waltz in silent dreams.
With every step, a tale is spun,
In the night, all fears undone.

Flickering lights that dance and play,
Guiding seekers who roam astray.
In whispered secrets, the night reveals,
The hidden truths that darkness heals.

In quiet moments, hearts entwine,
As dreams drift like a vintage wine.
In moonlit gardens, time stands still,
In perfect harmony, we feel the thrill.

So linger long in shadows' sway,
Let the moonlight lead the way.
For in this night, we become whole,
Embraced by dreams that heal the soul.

Milton Keynes UK
Ingram Content Group UK Ltd.
UKHW022343171124
451242UK00007B/115

9 789916 888568